Communication Skills

Social Skills & The Small Talk Challenge

Reid Damon

Social Skills

Build Confidence to Have a Conversation with Anyone by Managing Anxiety and Stress to Transform Your Personal and Professional Life.

DEDICATION

This book is dedicated to my wife Vee and daughter PJ. Thank you for your love and encouragement. I also want to dedicate this to people who want to be better. Life is short. Be your best.

Contents

Introduction

I want to thank you and **congratulate you** for reading this book, *Social Skills: Build Confidence to Have a Conversation with Anyone by Managing Anxiety and Stress to Transform Your Personal and Professional Life.*

This book contains proven steps and strategies on how to enrich your life by learning simple skills to have a conversation with anyone. You will learn the psychological reasons why we humans have anxiety and why we create mental fear when communicating with others.

Shyness, awkwardness, lack of conversational skills, and the inability to speak eloquently may cause self-doubt – thus crippling oneself.

After understanding those causes we will practice simple skill-building exercises that will develop your confidence. These simple steps will guide you in any social situation when speaking to a stranger, your boss, the opposite sex, or to anyone!

In addition, the entire book is laid out in a way that builds upon what you read and allows you to focus on **the most important social skills** – allowing you to slowly develop in a way that will not be intimidating. Keep an open mind and you'll learn the necessary skills to improve your personal and professional life.

Thanks again. I hope you enjoy it!

Warmest Regards,
Reid Damon

Chapter 1: Building Confidence Using Psychology

How can you build confidence in a way that will make sure you benefit from improved speech, better peer-to-peer relationships, and ever-improving control over how and what you say?

Unfortunately, confidence is not necessarily something that can be directly learned; rather having sufficient confidence to function properly in society is an **exercise of the mind** and the state that it currently is in, in addition to knowledge and skill.

An extension of confidence is **positive thinking**. In practice, you can train yourself based on the knowledge of your environment and the people you must interact with. When you do this you can ensure that confidence is being built. How?

Take a look at how you can quickly build confidence, which starts with TALKING to people all the time:

✓ **Start with the belief** that you can speak proficiently with all people. (Mind over matter). Try to believe it.

✓ **Think positively** and learn about your environment.

✓ **Practice in a full-length mirror** speaking to peers.

✓ **Experience feelings of well-being** and mindfulness.

✓ **Watch body positioning & gestures** as well as facial expressions.

Confidence extends from repetition when speaking with other people, belief and focus. You should start out with brief 5 to 10 second intervals of speaking to peers, and eventually ramp up to several minutes of relaxing and mindless fun conversation.

Try to talk to a variety of people at work and on your own free time. Gradually increase the time that you speak to people from a few seconds to a few minutes. You'll be able to feel more comfortable talking as time progresses.

Now we begin a simple skill-building exercise. Practice to *gently* change people's opinions about small things in conversation (recommend a restaurant, hobby, book etc.) or simply work together with other people in a productive manner.

1. Start with brief exchanges of simple and congenial things.

2. Be nice! Be friendly! Never say negative things at first.

3. Practice daily in a full-length mirror until you feel completely comfortable with brief exchanges.

4. Gauge the results and see how people are reacting to you and use this information to modify what you say the next time you see them.

The four simple steps above are a great way for **overly shy or nervous people** to begin to expand their aware-ness and use this information to share with coworkers and friends.

The act of sharing ideas with coworkers and friends allows you to grow your confidence and begin to expand your influence in your place of work, as well as with friends and family.

Ways to Improve Speaking & Focus

There are several different ways of improving speaking and gaining added focus. The primary goal of these methods is to build confidence and strengthen your skill set.

Here are some suggested concepts to get you up to speed:

Having conversations with strangers - if you've ever taken public speaking classes in college, one of the things they stress that you do is to **engage in conversation with complete strangers**. Obviously you want to do this at a time that is comfortable and convenient for both you and the individual you wish to practice your conversations with.

Most of us have no problem with at least speaking a few words to people because it is necessary in order to accomplish simple tasks in our society.

For example, most people feel comfortable speaking about the weather. There are infinite variations of the following conversation.

You: "Wow quite a rainstorm we had today, huh?"

Stranger: "Yeah, unbelievable."

You: "I was told that this weather would continue until next week. I suggest you stock up on essentials before all the stuff on the shelves disappear."

Stranger: "Yeah I guess I should become more prepared. I wish I knew a little bit more about that!"

The simple conversation above shows how easy it is to pick a topic that is of interest to most people and then introduce it as the topic for discussion.

Depending on someone's reaction, would determine whether or not you wish to continue with this line of conversation:

You: "You might be surprised to know disaster preparedness is my business. I don't typically talk about this to strangers but you seemed genuinely interested. Here is a business card and my website has all kinds of information about this."

Stranger: "Thanks, I will have a look. Nice meeting you."

Learning these skills will strengthen and improve relationships. It is quite possible for you to begin to enjoy the real fruits of your labor quickly – more clients for your business, a higher paying job or a better circle of friends.

Using speaking to make friends - the better speaker you become, the more you will be able to influence people around you. Then you can choose from the cream of the crop – the people whom you want to become closer to.

Public speaking, talking to strangers, having enjoyable and fun conversations with the people around you will practically ensure that you will generate improved quality friendships, as well as professional relationships.

Can you now see just exactly how simple it is to have a conversation with someone and hand a person a business card? In the above example simply engaging in conversation about the weather led to the speaker meeting a potential client.

The ability to speak in public can make all the difference in the world. Being able to approach people and have discussions means that you can influence them.

The real secret, especially when you're doing this professionally, is to gradually build confidence while talking with people.

For example, Michelle is shy, but wants to become an insurance agent. In order to successfully sell insurance you must be willing to speak to all different types of people from all walks of life.

Most people do not have the time or inclination to want to speak to strangers. It is your job to provide situations where you can accomplish this. From a professional standpoint, the ability to approach someone and bring him or her into a discussion means that you have control over them for a short period of time.

You should also understand that if you work in a profession that requires you to have contact with the public, you should take the time to practice and rehearse what you're going to say to people.

What you say to people should not sound robotic or mechanical either. These conversations are not genuine and do not build rapport. Work with other like-minded people in your industry and practice building confidence by rehearsing what you're going to say.

Chapter 2: Removing Doubt, Anxiety and Redirecting Your Power

Now you are aware of how easy it is to begin to build confidence through practicing public speaking. Next we're going to focus on redirecting your power and removing doubt and anxiety.

The first thing you should realize is that all people have doubts and many of these doubts can prevent you from accomplishing your goals. Doubts stem from our insecurities. How do we combat these insecurities?

We use **logic**.

Logic dictates that one of the best ways for removing doubt and anxiety is a process that has been referred to as **systematic desensitization.**

We are currently not practicing psychologists and will not get into all the mechanics of systematic desensitization. But we are going to take several steps out of this psychological tool and utilize them to help us remove doubt and anxiety:

✓ **Begin by practicing how you will behave** – what your body positioning and gestures will be like in a variety of different social situations. Practice, practice, and practice.

For example, Michelle has decided she will continue to practice her sales pitch for selling insurance. She decides to ask people if she can practice her insurance pitch on them to help her become a better salesperson.

This is an excellent tactic that most sales professionals use *to actually sell products* to people – by asking them to listen.

Systematic desensitization says that the best way to become unafraid in a process **is to confront it head-on** in steps until the issue no longer bothers you.

For example, Michelle is also afraid of spiders. A systematic desensitization process would gradually expose Michelle over time in a series of progressive and confrontational steps like this:

1. Michelle is shown several pictures of small spiders.

2. Michelle is taken into a room where there is a container filled with spiders.

3. Michelle is handed a sealed petri dish with several large spiders to handle and look at.

4. Michelle is given the petri dish with the lid off with a large spider to hold for a few seconds (spider is harmless).

5. Michelle holds a petri dish without the lid with a large spider for a minute, then two minutes.

6. Michelle places a large spider (harmless) in her hand.

As you can see, **the process involves a series of staged and progressive steps** for desensitizing yourself to a stimulus that induces anxiety, stress, fear and worry.

The exact same process is often used for public speaking as well as interacting with other people if you are shy or have fears.

This will help you prepare for dealing with anxiety and stress. As a result, over time your continuous exposure to any stimulus that is causing you discomfort will eventually pass. You are confronting it and defeating it in your mind.

This is an excellent way **to control anxiety** by creating a series of steps for public speaking or talking to others in a formal setting. The process may look something like this:

1. **You begin with researching public speaking** by looking at top public speakers and learning from them.

2. **You start practicing speaking in the mirror** until you begin to feel a bit more comfortable.

3. **You start talking to people at work for at least 1 minute** a day.

4. **You begin having 2 to 3 minute conversations** with people that respond positively to you.

5. **You give a small presentation at work** that lasts about 5 minutes and explains information from your department.

6. **You are asked to give a fairly large presentation** to officers of your business, this lasts about 20 minutes.

7. **You are chosen to give a one-hour presentation** as to why people should join the business you work for.

These steps are not exact to everyone's situation but provide you a guide to create your own steps that take you from being scared speechless, to systematically overcoming all anxiety and removing doubt.

When you remove doubt, you remove negative triggers that impede your ability to properly present information to other people. Over time, your public speaking skills will improve and you will be able to react and deliver information as well as maintain positive relationships.

Chapter 3: Removing Roadblocks from Your Life To Move Forward

Now that you understand the exact steps of how to desensitize yourself from anxiety and fears, it's time to focus on **removing roadblocks** from your life so you can move forward, guilt-free, fearless and focused.

Overcoming shyness can be accomplished by learning how to project your thoughts, feelings and ideas to other people effectively. Part of the systematic desensitization process is to pick the stimulus that is causing you the most concern, and then confront it head-on.

For example, Michelle is generally shy and doesn't like to speak up; she is usually the last person to say anything at business meetings.

Since Michelle knows it's important to overcome her shyness, she figures out a series of steps that she can do overtime to systematically give her back the control over her emotions and allow her to speak to her peers.

How to overcome a bad past – this is another area that people have problems with. For example, we learn that Steve grew up in a home where he was overly criticized whenever he spoke out about his thoughts.

Because of this, Steve became an introvert and doesn't like to speak in public. Steve now realizes that he needs to be able to speak to other people without fear or anxiety of being overly judged or criticized.

One of the best ways to deal with negative feelings is to first **clear your mind** and do **a series of deep breathing / relaxation techniques.**

By combining systematic desensitization with calming breathing exercises, you can maintain a state of calm and eventually overcome any fear.

Here are the steps to calming your mind and refocusing your energy on being peaceful, stress-free and ready to engage other people in productive conversation:

1. Start out by taking a slow, long and deep breath. As you take in the breath, feel your lungs being filled from inside with all the anxiety and negativity.

2. Exhale slowly, feeling all the negativity flow out of your body.

3. Take one deep breath and feel the positive energy and "goodness" fill your lungs.

4. Hold your breath for approximately 5 seconds and feel positive energy flowing into your body.

5. Breathe out again – feeling completely focused and happy.

This process (calming breath, negative energy out of your body, and feeling goodness returning back) will calm you by removing stress. It will help counteract issues in your past that may be preventing you from wanting to engage in productive public speaking or conversations with friends, family and work associates.

Whether you realize it or not, practicing this type of breathing several times a day – especially when you feel the most anxious and troubled – will have a powerful **biofeedback affect.**

Biofeedback is used during meditation and breathing exercises to reduce vital signs in people that are having stressful situations.

Studies show that this is highly effective at **controlling your emotions** and allowing you to regain mindfulness and focus.

This is a fabulous way to also manage stress before you speak. It will also allow you to increase personal relational skills so you can eventually command an audience.

Prior to any speech, you should practice controlling how you think, and focus on relaxing using this method.

This is a great time to take notes, prepare your presenta-tion, and even practice, by having conversations in a way that will have a positive impact on the people you're speaking to. For example, if Michelle was addressing senior citizens in an insurance presentation, she would modify her speech to reflect the points that are important to seniors, like retirement planning or long-term care.

Using Logic – Plato was quoted as saying that "*courage is knowing what not to fear*." I present this quote because it is at the core of creating confidence as well as the ability to work effectively with other people.

Being afraid, being shy, having doubts or anxiety is a result from lack of mental preparation and conditioning.

The good news is that logic is the ability to detach emotion and observe actually what is happening,

based solely on facts and proper inference as well as forming proper conclusions based on this information.

People that are capable of using logic can never be controlled by their emotions. Even if you are a passionate person who is often affected by emotions – a quick series of deep breathing exercises can remove the emotion and allow you to make a decision based on logic.

Logic will allow you to be unrestricted by emotion thus strengthening your ability to connect with people.

One of the best ways to use logic is to view your mind as a scale, and to add facts onto each side of the scale. Whatever the outcome, it should be most likely the choice that you make.

For example, Jason works at a convenience store. He is told that if he sells the most 52 ounce soda drinks today he will win a $25 prize. Other employees don't like asking every customer if they would like to purchase a fountain drink. Jason realizes that logically, if he offers a fountain drink to everyone who comes into the store, especially if other employees are not doing so, there is a very good chance that he will win the contest.

Here is a way to use logic effectively:

✓ **Get the facts** – regardless of the emotions that people experience, logic allows you to see through the cloud of emotion. When you are capable of doing this, you can make logical decisions based on facts and not feelings.

✓ **Base your decisions on what is best** – it may be interesting or even exciting to tell your boss to shove it; but the next day you have to go out and get another job! Watch what you say and how you handle your emotions by functioning almost exclusively on logic. It will change your life!

✓ **Remember when you're using logic not to become a cold fish**! You certainly can be positive, happy and fun-loving with people *while* making solid decisions in your life by relying on the facts and logic.

Using logic to make your decisions while backing it up with positive emotions will allow you *to speak to almost anyone and discern the correct information* necessary for a success.

Ultimately your job will require you to have the skills so practicing them now will allow you to continue to expand your consciousness and awareness of events around you.

Relational techniques can drive conversations in a direction that will benefit you. Remember that all people are driven and/or governed by three primary forces:

✓ **Emotions** – most people cannot control them.

✓ **Desires** – we all have them and some people let them get out of control. It reaches a point that they are driven exclusively by emotion and desire.

✓ **Intellect** – this is the cold and/or calculating part of us that can differentiate between emotions and desires. This is similar to the id that governs the ego and superego with the id as a bridge. Utilizing intellect is your best bet when it comes to controlling your emotions and your desires.

Conversations that start with a small amount of emotion such as discussing with others their likes/desires are wonderful ways to utilize these relational techniques. This type of topic can fuel any conversation you want to have.

It is easy to start a conversation. One of the best examples is discussing the weather with people – especially if it is rather serious weather. You can utilize the same techniques of focusing on emotions, desires and intellect so that you can effectively start and then manage any conversation.

Chapter 4: Powerful Social Skills of Top Performers and How To Learn Them Now

One of the best ways to become successful in life is to focus powerful social skills and use them to rise in prominence.

Whether you are aware of it or not, many of the top CEOs, professionals, business executives and politicians all rely on the ability to speak eloquently and expertly.

This is a skill that is used by these people to achieve success. They also use their confidence and social skills to help guide and influence others.

There are some people that just naturally exhibit skills that the rest of us have to work at; yet in reality we discover that some of the top speakers in the world learned their skills the same way you might learn a new sport or language. Practice, practice and more practice.

The focus of this discussion centers on charisma and how it can manifest. Charisma is the ability of someone using their personality to influence other people to behave in a certain way.

For example, **_Dr. Martin Luther King Jr._** was universally respected and loved. He was thought to be one of the world's best charismatic speakers.

There certainly are other examples of how charisma can be used to influence and lead people. We will cover more examples later in this chapter.

The first step to build charisma is to fully understand the audience that you are engaging. Then you must prepare a proper presentation. The last step will be to practice it until the speech flows naturally. This is a key step that needs to be repeated and repeated.

There's an old saying: _"prior proper planning prevents this poor performance!"_ In other words, taking the time to thoroughly prepare and practice is the most critical element to giving a proper presentation.

Personality, strength of character, and the ability to use variations in tone are also very important to commanding an audience.

There are common attributes seen in top professional and political speakers. They have a cadence and rhythm, as well as a process that they follow in order to project charisma.

Here are eight simple ways to entice your audience:

✓ **Thoroughly know the material** and the possible questions that such content will elicit from your audience.

✓ **Practice the speech frequently** and make sure that you know the information so well that it literally flows over the tip of your tongue.

✓ **Understand your audience** by thoroughly researching the kind of information that they look forward to hearing. Make sure that you're going to say things that people respond to well.

✓ **Always appear natural and relaxed** and start off your speech slow and with a gentle and simple cadence.

✓ **Begin to pick up the tempo** and start adding emotion into your voice as you make points.

✓ **Increase your energy and become more animated** as you use proper gestures to emphasize the points that you are making.

- ✓ **Use emotions to get people to listen more intently** and begin drawing people into the emotional whirlwind that you create.

- ✓ **Deliver critical and shocking information** but information that you know people want to hear. Make your biggest points when you have raised the tempo of your speech.

Of course there are many other important points when it comes to invoking charisma, but these are the most important ones and something that anyone can master with practice.

Now you understand the process behind invoking charisma. The next step is to see how persuasive speeches are presented.

If you truly wish to understand how charisma works, it is important to look at a majority of the world's best charismatic speakers. **Please take some time and search the internet** for "great speeches" by Dr. Martin Luther King Jr., John F. Kennedy, Winston Churchill and Barack Obama, just to name a few.

Don't just listen to their speeches **but actually get copies of the speeches and practice them** in the same manner that some of the top speakers in the world have done.

The idea is to stand on the shoulders of geniuses and learn prismatic speech by following in the footsteps of some of the greatest public speakers the world has ever seen.

When you master even parts of these kinds of persuasive speeches, you will notice improvements in your professional and personal life. This will allow you to succeed by the force of your personality, and by the ability to express information that people want to hear.

This will also allow you to be more likeable because people will actually want to gravitate towards you. You can also gain people's trust quickly by focusing on always speaking the truth.

Telling the truth is essentially a revolutionary act today because so many people make up facts and lie. Being an honest and truthful person is a reward unto itself because people will automatically begin to trust you. When people trust you, it will be far easier to lead them.

Here's an example of how you can influence people simply by using your spoken word:

- ✓ Steve gives a speech on the importance of safe food handling to a group of professional restaurant entrepreneurs (authority building).

✓ Steve is now viewed as an expert on the subject. Several entrepreneurs approach for additional information after the speech (business opportunities).

✓ Steve gives additional handouts that provide valuable follow-up information that can save restaurant owners a fortune from foodborne illness claims (powerful info.)

✓ People in Steve's industry are happy because he is saving them large amounts of money (people like him).

✓ Now when Steve visits and gives additional speeches, he is able to get more restaurant entrepreneurial clients who need his training for the staff (grow his business).

✓ Steve will make many friends and influence this industry by simply emitting the power of his persuasive speech.

So just by presenting valuable information to others in a speech, Steve gets experience, leads, business associates and friends. Not a bad deal here.

Chapter 5: Mind Over Matter

There are powerful psychological constructs that can help people gain control over their **subconscious mind** in order to create almost anything you might want to accomplish in life.

This is because psychologists have learned **that the subconscious mind cannot differentiate between reality and fantasy** and is simply a storehouse of reactive information that has been learned and stored for quick reference.

You can teach your subconscious that you want to eat healthy foods and that you cannot eat anymore excess junk food. Over time your subconscious will store this data and then act on your conscious behavior over time as psychological cues accrue.

This is one of the ways that a psychologist can either pre-program someone or de-program them, contingent on the kind of behavior that they wish to project.

Whether you're aware of it or not, developing social skills also requires you to condition your subconscious. The conditioning will help you to avoid self sabotage.

Your conscious mind may have between 10,000 to 20,000 thoughts a day. It is estimated that the subconscious mind can have up to 100,000 unique thoughts a day. That is five to ten times more frequent than your conscious mind!

Properly conditioning your subconscious mind is like filling in a new database on a computer with millions of small snippets of events that occur throughout your day and are triggered automatically. The subconscious works on this "stored data".

Your subconscious mind has an effect over your behavior. Consider what happens to people that go to see a horror movie. When the bad guy or monster attacks one of the characters in the movie – we all jump! We do this knowing full well that we are watching a movie that is not real.

Your subconscious mind is programmed with millions of psychological cues that cause it to react very much in the same way.

What is the first thing that you do if a bug lands on your arm? Brush it away immediately or even slap it? Again, we are talking about a programmed response that happens almost automatically.

Numerous psychologists have written dozens of white papers explaining that if you take the time to present information to your subconscious (i.e. a vision board) you can actually change your behavior and allow your conscious thoughts to eventually control most of your subconscious behavior.

For some people this is a breath of fresh air, and an amazing revelation because now it is quite possible to program yourself for success!

You will gain the ability to alter negative behavior over time by using deep embeds (sleep tapes, vision boards, meditation and thought programming).

For example, Steve grew up in an abusive home and he gained a lot of weight as a child. Through his adult life he has been struggling with weight gain until finally he began to program his subconscious mind by showing himself daily images of his face on a slender and fit male body.

He also created a vision board with positive affirmations to support this new change in habits. Steve finally began to lose large amounts of weight and finally kept it off over the many months by programming his subconscious. He was no longer self-sabotaging.

This can be referred to as: "preprogramming" which helps you master all social skills by projecting these skills into your subconscious. How do you do that? By creating positive affirmations, as well as a vision board, will allow you to focus your mind on the reasons why you're trying to succeed at mastering your life.

Please search the internet for "positive affirmations" and "vision boards". See how people use these tools to focus their subconscious mind. This step will help provide inspiration when you create your own positive affirmations and vision boards.

Chapter 6: Social Mastery 101

In this section we are going to explore the importance of social mastery *when it comes to practicing the skills with other people*, or as psychologists like to refer to it: "working in the field".

You should practice each of these three points daily in order to increase your social skills. *The third and final point is broken down into actual steps*. The exercises below are some of the best so stay focused and see just how well your social skills blossom:

- ✓ **Breathing exercises** to remove anxiety, stress and fear. We have already discussed the importance of following the steps that we provided earlier in this book. Breathing exercises also increase your stamina and ability to speak from the diaphragm. Do not skip this important step.

- ✓ **Meditation** is critical to overall health and wellness, and regular meditation can reduce stress and help you to manage anxiety – resulting in a clear and focused mindset.

✓ **How to master basic conversations** using the formula **MGARID** (Meet, Greet, Associate, Redress, Interest, Detach). This acronym can help you remember all the things you need to do in order to get along with people and have productive conversations without feeling shy, introverted or uninvolved.

MGARID By Steps

Here is step three broken down into manageable snippets:

Meet - here is where you break the ice by being congenial, pleasant and smiling. Your first meeting is important so look people directly in the eye, shake their hand firmly and thank them for their time. This is the accepted method in business.

Greet - greeting is different than meeting because you must also deliver a message. When you meet someone you simply say hello and shake his or her hand firmly while presenting positive body language. The next stage is when you have to greet someone. Greeting is an extended and a more focused interactive setting. If you're required to greet people formally –introduce yourself as well as expressing your pleasure at meeting them.

Associate – here you are trying to work with a colleague, friend or family member and you must constantly interact in a positive and uplifting manner. Most people associate with like-minded people and are rewarded by their friendship. Some of the best rewards are simply pleasant comments and compliments.

Redress – during the course of interacting and associating with people, occasionally you may say something that offends people. Redressing means accepting ownership for anything negative that you've done and offering some kind of emotional, physical, or psychological enticement. For example, you take a group of people out to dinner and pay for it because you missed a prior meeting with them.

Interest – slowly draw people into your life by following the interests of other people and emulating those interests yourself. For example, Steve found out that the district manager loves to play basketball. Steve calls the district manager and says he loves playing basketball too and would like to join the company team.

Detach – not everybody you meet will want to be your friend or associate. That is ok. Do not force or be overly aggressive in building relationships. You do not want to cause additional harm or strain to the relationship. Also it is often a good idea to take a step back from people who appear to be harmful or destructive in your life – even if these people are family members. You must evaluate whether or not the relationship is worth your time.

All of the steps above do not necessarily occur in the exact order that they've been presented; but each is an important function of how to navigate through social situations in your life.

It is important that you take the opportunity to practice your skills at as many social functions as you can attend. It is similar to gaining and building skills at any job that you do. Attending all forms of social functions will ensure that you get lots of practice.

You will have a good command over social events once you have completed all of these other steps. The last series of steps is exactly how you should prepare for any form of public speaking:

1. Know your audience and what they like and do not like.

2. Prepare a list of important bullet points for your speech.

3. Write your speech and make sure the information is accurate, interesting and focused to the specific audience you are engaging.

4. Begin practicing your speech in a full-length mirror until you can deliver all of the information while only briefly glancing at your bullet points.

5. Once you feel comfortable with your speech – have someone record you so you can review what portions can be improved. Stay positive! Do not dwell on the corrections. Feel good about the process.

6. Make corrections to your speech and record it again until it is almost flawless.

7. Practice, practice, practice! Never sound like you are reading to an audience. Notes are meant to keep you on track. Only use it as a guide.

8. Consult the charisma section and follow the steps to actively deliver a powerful speech that will have people spellbound!

Once again, I remind you to thoroughly investigate some of the top public speakers in the world because they will teach you many tactics. Your delivery and the ability to involve people directly in the information that you are providing are key aspects in building charisma and a successful speech.

Real Life Uses for These Techniques

In this last section we are going to provide practical applications for using this information in everyday life. Our goal is to put *the actual techniques* you have learned into practice to help improve three important facets of life:

- ✓ **Your personal relationships** by quantifying how you want them to be and how you can change and improve these relationships.

- ✓ **Your professional relationships** by also quantifying goals and beginning to achieve better influence and outcomes at work.

- ✓ **Your gender-specific cues** that you can use contingent if you are male or female. While the techniques work well regardless of your gender, **there are nuances that can help magnify your success when dealing with the opposite sex.**

These are three important types of relationships, and we will cover each. We will start with **your personal relationships.**

Before we can offer any advice, you need to first do *an evaluation or baseline* on all three aspects of concern – personal, professional and gender cues.

A baseline is observable information that you record for a time frame to help you decide what techniques would work best to change relationships in your life.

For example, Lisa knows her relationship with her mother has been strained for years. She wants to correct it. She decides to observe her and her mother's behaviors for one month. She records every exchange she has with her mother for later analysis.

Lisa uses a notebook to record their conversations and actions (after the meeting, call or exchange). Lisa writes the entries in as much detail as possible:

- ✓ How she talks to her mother, including the tone of her voice and what she says.

- ✓ How her mother responds and her reactions to what is said.

- ✓ The situations and timing when Lisa and her mother interact and her feelings at that moment.

✓ What actual behavior she uses with her mother.

✓ What actual behavior her mother uses with her.

At the end of the month Lisa evaluates how she did with her mother. Now she has information about why she cannot get along with her mother. Lisa notices that most of the strain is about a lack of overall respect between the two of them.

Lisa is following this baseline to see what is going on:

✓ When do negative feelings happen that make you not want to be in your mother's presence? What triggers these feelings?

✓ When are the moments that you like being in her presence and vice versa?

Once you can elicit these two observations, you can now use **Behavior Modification** to eliminate the negative occurrences and use positive reinforcement to construct better exchanges.

Behavior Modification relies on measurable behavior. You need to track what you do and see the results.

Lisa realizes it is her own lack of respect for her mother that hinders their relationship. Lisa begins to use **positive reinforcement** (R+ is the symbol psychologists use) as a tool of Behavior Modification.

Positive reinforcement states that a behavior will occur more (i.e. Lisa and her mother getting along) if it is reinforced by something people really like and want. For example if you want a dog to sit, you can teach the dog using a treat or reward to positively reinforce the behavior until it occurs more frequently.

Lisa knows her mother just wants more respect so she devises **a schedule of respectful contact** (R+) with her mother. Lisa shows her respect at least three times a week by taking her out to lunch, shopping and going to her favorite garden shops.

Within a few weeks Lisa and her Mother are no longer at odds.

Your professional relationships can be improved as well by using this tool if you interact enough with them. Treating coworkers like friends, as long as no lines are crossed, is always a great way to help bring people together.

When working with people other than your family or close friends, one of the best ways to influence people is to remember the information from the "Removing Roadblocks" section. All people are influenced (and even controlled) by several factors:

Emotions - most people cannot control them or are controlled by them.

Desires - we all have them and some people are driven exclusively by emotion and desire.

Intellect - this is the cold and/or calculating part that can differentiate between emotions and desires. People use intellect to justify their emotional decisions.

Using the three behavioral cues above, you can focus on what other people think or desire and align yourself with them. Once aligned, you can influence their actions, decisions and even influence them to do things they might not normally do.

For example, Lisa realizes that her coworker, John, loves the San Francisco 49ers. Lisa sees the EMOTION and DESIRE in his eyes when he talks about the team. Many of her coworkers including herself are clueless about football. Lisa also notices that not many people care that John likes the 49ers.

She sees a big San Francisco 49ers coffee cup at the store and buys it for John. She hopes to build a deeper relationship with him so she can join the office "coffee clique" that John seems to control. Having John as a closer associate will benefit her job. With a simple gift, she is accepted into the elite office clique!

The key to influencing people is to become *more like them in behavior* and to agree with people on most of what they think, feel and appreciate.

This is called **"Cognitive Tuning"** and allows you to be on the same page or frequency of the people you want to relate to.

Remember, be nice, agree to like what others do (at least at work) and when in Rome, do as the Romans do. I am not asking you to be untrue to yourself. Be you throughout the process.

I want you to treat this process like a game. You need to take certain steps to win. This is a necessary step for Cognitive Tuning.

Remember the process for "how to speak with associates"?

- ✓ Start with brief exchanges of simple and congenial things.

- ✓ Be nice! Be friendly! Never say negative things.

- ✓ Gauge the results and see how people are reacting to you. Use this information to modify what you say the next time you see them.

Influencing people at work is a slow and progressive process that takes time. It is like playing a game where every exchange is carefully calculated but appears natural, supportive, friendly and consistent.

Making friends means that you must now view people in *"Unconditional Positive Regard"*. No matter what someone says or does to you – always, ALWAYS be positive, friendly and concerned.

Over time, human nature will drive people to you in droves. People LOVE other people who love and want to be like them. Always project positivity because people are psychologically addicted to how good they feel about themselves when they are around you.

Be the bringer of joy and goodness in people's lives. You must be a force for good, and with this energy comes the ability to positively change your life and everyone else's life around you.

Many studies have been done on people with the ability to emote positive emotions, positive desires and intellectual support in their lives. You will become a powerful influence and people will not be able to help themselves.

Of course this does not mean you should let people walk all over you, or be nice to them regardless of anything they do to you. You simply can't lose if you can always be the focus of good feelings!

People will have to listen to you because their own ego is so caught up in your opinions. This powerful secret can change your life forever!

Gender roles – why are we discussing gender roles as the final point in this book? This is because there are differing ways men and women think. You must understand and behave in a way that works well with the opposite sex.

There are obviously exceptions to what I say here about the genders; and these are simply constructs for thought:

Women – Most women tend to see the world through the filter of emotion. Women are hardwired to focus on family, relationships, children, siblings and all things beautiful.

Women love to be in nature and are affected more by inter-personal relationships. Women make incredible caregivers, nurturers and organizers.

Men – Most men tend to see the world through the filter of logic. Men are tinkerers, motor heads and sports fans. They love competition and the clash of the gladiatorial swords in the arena of life.

Men are all warriors at heart and even the weakest man believes he can win under the right circumstances. Men relate the best to other guys – first and foremost.

If you decide to talk to a man and you are a woman you should know a few things:

- ✓ Men tend to listen to women who are friendly to them.

- ✓ Men believe you will date them under certain circumstances.

- ✓ Men want to protect and nurture women.

- ✓ Men want lots of female friends, if possible.

- ✓ Men believe in straight-talk and do not like long-winded and overly superfluous speech.

As a woman, knowing these things about men can allow you to structure how to talk to them for maximum benefit.

For example, Lisa knows that John likes a woman who is straightforward and speaks directly. She walks up to him and puts two tickets to the 49ers game on his desk. Lisa says, "John. Pick you up at 9:00AM on Sunday buddy."

This ***blows John away*** and he readily agrees. What a woman that Lisa is! John is hooked. When is the last time a woman asked a man to a football game and paid for the tickets? Psychology works . . .

If you decide to talk to a woman and you are a man you should know a few things:

- ✓ Women tend to listen to men who are social, chatty and project a warm and sensitive perspective.

- ✓ Women believe you will do anything to sleep with them and use this to get what they want, even if the man doesn't want to sleep with them.

- ✓ Women want a man who can provide for them materially, emotionally and physically.

- ✓ Women tend to have more conversations about their feelings, beliefs, emotions and issues in their lives.

- ✓ Women love to share emotionally charged stories that tend to have moral implications that support their circle of friends.

As you can see, women are much more involved in an emotional and relational hierarchy with other women. The best way for any man to approach and integrate into a group like this is to do the following:

✓ A man will need to prove he is of good moral character as women work in packs to protect the group of women.

✓ Once a man is invited into the group of females he must be SUBMISSIVE or he will be ostracized quickly.

✓ Men must be like a knight in shining armor and NEVER "hit on" any of the females.

✓ Men must bring something to the group of girls that they need, and he must be KIND to every woman in the group.

Men need to follow the hierarchy of women and build a relationship with the alpha female in any work environment. For example, Steve notices Michelle looking at him frequently. You know Michelle has substantial influence over others in the office. She has made several suggestions to him that they could discuss work at the local coffee shop.

Steve decides to take her up on her offer. They meet after work and they talk for hours. During this time Lisa walks over and joins them.

Steve stands up and pulls the chair out for Lisa and seems happy she showed up (actually he is annoyed for the interruption but NEVER shows this).

Steve is a complete gentleman and buys both ladies a coffee.

He listens to the girls talk and only speaks when the conversation shifts to him. He also compliments both women on how smart they are at work and he hopes to learn from them. Steve offers to share his expertise from his department in order to make both of their jobs easier.

When Steve goes to the men's room, Lisa gives two thumbs up to Michelle. Good job Steve! You used the list above to "get in good" with the people running the office. A few months later, Steve is promoted to office manager . . .

Using your tools in this guide and following all of these steps can help you finally cut through the red tape and finally create relationships that matter.

Regardless if you are a man or woman, now you know exactly what to do for almost any situation when dealing with family, friends and associates. Use the steps herein but temper what you do or say based on the gender differences. Once you get to know the person better, you can simply use **unconditional positive regard** at all times in order to deepen friendships.

More on unconditional positive regard – this is a client-based therapy created by renowned psychologist Carl Rogers.

This is a form of therapy that is used to develop **a relationship with the client and the user**. The reason this therapy is so powerful is that it allows no restriction between people. Relationships will happen and continue to grow.

Carl Rogers spoke of **tapping the hidden resources inside all people** and that this can only be done if people are 100% positive regardless of what the person says, does or believes:

"People also nurture our growth by being accepting – by offering us what Rogers called unconditional positive regard. **This is an attitude of grace, an attitude that values us even knowing our failings**. It is a profound relief to drop our pretenses, confess our worst feelings, and discover that we are still accepted. In a good marriage, a close family, or an intimate friendship, we are free to be spontaneous without fearing the loss of others' esteem."

Source: David G. Myers, *Psychology: Eighth Edition*

Unconditional positive regard may be the most potent tool in your arsenal that will allow you to shape your relationships. The tool breaks down barriers, and allows people from all walks of life to relate and become friends. It can be used in almost any situation where you might have a conflict.

For example, Joe waits in line at his local café for his morning coffee. Just then, a harried looking businessman knowingly steps in front of him and begins ordering a coffee.

Joe can react several ways:

- ✓ Tell the guy who cut ahead in line to get to the back of the line.

- ✓ Joe can ignore the man and just forget it.

- ✓ Joe could react favorably and make a point.

Joe decides on the last step. He decides to act positively rather than negatively. Joe clears his throat and offers to buy his coffee:

"Hey you must really be in a hurry! Ma'am can I pay for his coffee and mine at the same time?"

The man is stunned and even embarrassed so he thanks Joe. Later that week he sees the guy again and the man approaches him: "Sir, I remember you being so nice to me. I heard you talking to the girl at the coffee stand; and I heard you were looking for a job downtown. Well I need someone like you!"

Creating positive experiences like this and helping people (not overreacting) while keeping your cool will always pay off. This step may sound crazy to some people. Keep an open mind!

Stay positive! You will see how greatly a positive attitude can influence your ability to speak to people.

Conclusion

Thank you again for reading this book!

You have already started your first steps in changing your life. I hope this book was able to help you understand why we feel anxiety and stress in social situations. You have also completed these simple lessons that will guide you for a lifetime. These steps will take practice, patience, and an open mind to achieve.

The next step is to change another part of your life that has been hindering your happiness and self-development. For example, it may be to quit smoking in order to better your health.

It might be losing weight and exercising – leading to you running your first marathon. It can be you learning a new language and then moving and living in a new country.

It can be you quitting your job and starting a new career in something you love! You can achieve anything you set your mind to. Life is full of surprises.

You never know what one can achieve if one doesn't try.

Lucky for you, you've already tried and succeeded. Now take on the world head-on. Good luck! See you on the road to a better you. Thank you again!

Finally, if you enjoyed this book, then I'd like to ask you for a favor; would you be kind enough to leave a review for this book on Amazon? It'd be greatly appreciated!

Thank you and good luck!

Conversation

The Small Talk Challenge

7 Simple Steps to Learn How to Talk to People

monetary loss due to the information herein, either directly or indirectly.

Respective authors own all copyrights not held by the publisher.

The information herein is offered for informational purposes solely, and is universal as so. The presentation of the information is without contract or any type of guarantee assurance.

The trademarks that are used are without any consent, and the publication of the trademark is without permission or backing by the trademark owner. All trademarks and brands within this book are for clarifying purposes only and are the owned by the owners themselves, not affiliated with this document.

Dedication

This book is dedicated to my wife Vee and daughter PJ. Thank you for your love and encouragement. Also, a big thank you to all my readers and fans. Your passion in self development and improvement keeps me motivated and propels me forward in life.

Table of Contents

Introduction

I want to thank you and congratulate you for reading the book, *Conversation: The Small Talk Challenge: 7 Simple Steps to Learn How to Talk to People.*

This book contains proven steps and strategies on how to have a conversation with anyone. These steps are meant to be easy and fun so make sure to HAVE FUN!

Starting conversations, that is, the ability to connect with people so strongly that you end up creating a bond and thus, a thriving social network, is one of the keys to living a successful life. When you think about it, how many times have you heard or seen people use their connections to get ahead in life?

For instance, if you are jobless, and you hear of a work opportunity that fits your exact expertise at a firm where your friend works, would you not use that connection to get the job, to learn as much as you can about the job and the company offering it? You will have firsthand information of the intricacies of the job opening. Your advantage of knowing someone within the company will come in handy when you go for that interview. As this illustrates, the power of having a thriving social network has many implications on your life.

Those who have a good social network are those who have mastered the art of conversation. They have mastered their fear of talking to strangers and learned how to engage anyone in a conversation. A conversation at a bar, the beach, the train, a shared cab or even a chance meeting at a concert can lead to a lifelong relationship (or in some cases, a life partner), a meeting of minds or even a thriving business partnership.

If you lack the ability to strike up conversations, especially with people you don't know, you will be hindering your personal growth. You never know. The person you are afraid of saying hi to could be the person who changes your life. He or she could be your next business partner, life partner, or even greatest friend. If you are always cowering, allowing the fear of talking to strangers wash over, and control you, you are doing yourself a disservice.

Would you like to learn how to overcome the challenge of being unable to speak to people, especially strangers? Would you like to learn how to talk to anyone and experience the sense of fun, excitement, and accomplishment that comes with creating new connections? If you would, you are in for a treat because while being a great conversationalist requires effort and practice, this book has distilled everything you need to know into 7 simple steps to go from *"I can't talk to strangers"* to *"I can't wait for a chance to talk to and interact with everyone."*

The challenging nature of the steps vary from the first being the easiest and the last being the most difficult. If you read this guide and implement what you learn, you will gain the ability to talk to anyone! Are you up to the challenge?

There is a notes section after each action step. Document each interaction to track your progress. This will allow you to examine what worked and what didn't. Each interaction may not turn out the way you imagined. Don't feel discouraged. These steps may take time until you feel comfortable especially if these are new concepts to you. The most important thing to remember is to stay positive and have fun!

Thanks again for reading this book. I hope you enjoy it!

Warmest Regards,

Reid Damon

Step 1: Overcome the Fear of Speaking to People

In most instances, and this is something you might relate to, the fear of speaking to people, especially people you do not know, comes from learned values. Our parents and society teach children to be afraid of strangers. While this is good for safety reasons, unfortunately, instead of growing out of it, because of the strong emotions tied to its enforcement, many of us subconsciously ferry this belief into our adult lives.

This belief becomes so automatic that it is unknown to us. It influences how many people we interact with; think about it. Why is it that even though many of us travel on buses, trains, and airport shuttles, rarely do any of us talk to the stranger seated next to us? Not only do we not talk to the person, we rarely utter a simple hello. Why do you think that is?

It is because after many years of enforcing the "fear strangers" belief, the belief has become so automatic that even when seated next to someone, when our mind says, "Come on! Say hi," we quash it with thoughts such as "mind your own business. No one wants to hear what you have to say."

To become a great conversationalist, you need to overcome the fear of talking to strangers. To do this, you need to understand that the fear of talking to strangers often comes from the fear of rejection: being so fearful that once you say hi, the person on the other end is going to reject you.

What you should realize right now is that this fear has no grounding. It is an unfounded fear and while rejection can hurt, if you detach yourself from the fear of rejection, especially rejection from people you have never met before, you will easily overcome this fear. This understanding will overwrite your previous mindset.

You will now apply this knowledge to two techniques detailed below. The combination of methods will help alleviate the fear of engaging strangers in conversation. Let us discuss these now:

1: The Mindset Hack Technique

To overcome the fear of talking to strangers, you need to hack your mindset because your mindset towards conversations with strangers is what makes you fearful, nervous and anxious (this goes back to the fear of rejection).

To hack your mindset, the first thing you need to do is acknowledge that the fear of rejection is nothing but a perceived fear, which is something we discussed earlier. In addition, because such a fear is negative, you need to minimize the occurrence of negative thoughts and emotions. This goes back to, whenever you want to start a conversation with a stranger, you hear thoughts such as "leave the person be," or "no one cares about what you have to say."

The best thing to do is to draw three deep diaphragmatic breaths, and once you feel centered and calm, which is the effect you shall experience, concentrate on the positive outcome of the conversation. Perhaps the other person wants to say hi but because like you, he or she is caught in a negative thought loop. "No, I can't." If you break the ice, the person on the other end of the conversation will open up to the conversation and before you know it, you are chatting like old friends.

2: The Outward Focus Technique

Our minds have a tendency of blowing the fear of conversing with strangers out of proportion. To overcome this, be mindful of yourself, where you are, and the person you are about to engage in conversation. However, instead of concentrating on your internal dialog of how talking to a stranger who may or may not reject you is such a bad idea, concentrate on noticing and marking various things about the person you are about to say hi to.

It is rather unfortunate that we have accepted the notion that "starting a conversation is hard." This notion and the perceived difficult nature of starting a conversation with strangers relates to the chosen methodology.

Instead of concentrating inward on coming up with a witty conversation starter, focus outward by observing the person you want to engage in conversation — in a non-creepy way of course — and notice the little details. Analyzing how a person looks or behaves is key. Then you try to come up with conversation starter ideas based on your observations.

Here is an example. If you are boarding an airport shuttle and the crew is helping you and one other passenger load your luggage, by observing the other person, you may notice that she has a suitcase or earrings similar to yours. This is a great way to break past your fear of rejection and at the same time, start a great conversation (naturally, we are less likely to reject those who we have some similarity with).

Action Step

The next time you find yourself seated next to a stranger, take deep breaths, and calm your racing mind. To overcome the fear of conversing with strangers, remember that even if the person rejects you, the earth shall continue revolving on its axis. To make it impossible for the person to reject you, focus on the similarities between the two of you — something as simple as similar sneakers will do and you can use this as a conversation starter. Remember, this is supposed to be fun!

Like most people struggling with talking to strangers, you may be struggling with making a proper introduction. Let us look more closely into this in the next step.

Notes:

_Keep practicing…

Step 2: Learn How to Make a Proper Introduction

Introducing yourself to someone you have never met is often the hardest part of being in a conversation with strangers. Rarely will you hear someone say, "Oh how I love the excitement of walking up to strangers and introducing myself." Most of us are very apprehensive about introducing ourselves to strangers.

If you have yet to implement the previous step, you should do it right now. You should first overcome the two common obstacles to a proper introduction — the fear of rejection and an inward focus — before moving to step 2.

Now that you have overcome these two obstacles, the next thing on your to-do list is to learn how to introduce yourself to strangers whether at a cocktail party, the train, restaurant, or anywhere. Here are the various things you need to do:

Be Bold and Take the Initiative

Have you ever noticed how when we walk into new places where we know no one, we stand to the side and start assessing — with prejudice — the strangers to determine who seems friendly and approachable? This is why, for instance, when you attend a networking event, you will see tons of people pressed against the wall with phone in hand and heads bowed. The same applies to a public area such as the train. You will notice many seated at the corner or edges of their seats with their heads down or focused on other things.

Instead of following suit, boldly walk into any room or area full of strangers with confidence while assessing who looks interesting. Now use the outward focus strategy we discussed in step 1 to look for people you have a commonality with.

Another great trick is to look for cues that signal an interesting conversation ahead. For instance, if you are attending a networking event where everyone looks crisp and clean dressed in a suit and tie, and you notice someone in a beach shirt and flip-flops, this could be the signal for a great conversation because this person must have an interesting reason for going against the grain.

Once you find such a person, because many people are cagey about introducing themselves, center yourself and gather the courage to say a hello. This brings us to the next topic …

Shake Hands or Say Hello

The easiest way to introduce yourself is to offer your hand for a greeting or say hello. Extending your hand for a greeting is better because it makes you seem approachable, warm, friendly, and confident. This may seem like an awkward step, but we have been trained subconsciously to reciprocate a handshake when another person extends his/her hand. This has become an accepted line of social interaction so don't fear. However, if your hands are perspiring, something relatively common in those afraid of conversing with strangers, you can say hello and continue the conversation from there.

As you shake hands, resist the temptation to squeeze the hand too tightly. In no one's mind is a crushing handshake enjoyable. In the same breath, do not offer a limp handshake, what we call a wet fish handshake because such a handshake speaks of low confidence. Aim to strike a balance between the two.

Maintain Eye Contact

This is the most important part of approaching a stranger. Walk into a room, scan and notice a stranger you would like to engage in conversation. As you walk towards that person to introduce yourself with a handshake, hello, and some pleasantries, maintain eye contact especially if the person is looking at you as you approach. This will portray confidence, which will draw the interest of the other person.

Moreover, as you shake the person's hand, maintain eye contact. This shows you are present and ready for an interesting interaction. Other than humanizing yourself, good eye contact allows you to read body language cues that you can then use to create rapport (we shall talk about this in step 5).

Attentively Listen

Nervousness causes many to monopolize a conversation, ramble or even over talk. For example, if you are anxious and nervous, after shaking someone's hand and saying something like "Hi, I'm X or Y," you may blubber on without giving the person a chance to introduce him or herself to you. This does not bode well in fostering a good conversation. Feeling heard is a core human need. If you deny the other person a chance to discuss the things he or she cares about, the conversation you are trying to start will be over before you get past the pleasantries.

After saying hi and introducing yourself by name, give the other person a chance to reciprocate and once the person tells you his or her name, remember it and use it during the conversation.

Using these four strategies, you can introduce yourself to anyone.

Action Step

Take the initiative: introduce yourself to that interesting stranger by offering a firm handshake and as you start up the conversation, maintain eye contact, listen attentively, and respond with open-ended questions that draw the conversation further.

The sad thing is that most of us do not know what to say after the introduction. This is where small talk comes in. The next step teaches you how to master the art of small talk.

Notes:

_____

_____

_____

_____

_____

_____

_____

_____

_____

_____

_____

_____

_____

_____

_____

_____

_____

_____

_____

_____

_____

_____

_____

_____

_____

_____

_____

_____

Keep practicing…

Step 3: Master the Art of Small Talk

The beginning of a conversation is like the initial spark/ignition that brings an engine to life. Just as the engine needs fuel to continue roaring, after the introductions, your conversation with a stranger needs fuel to keep going. This is what we call small talk.

Small talk is how you get the conversation started and how you propel it into deeper topics. When it comes to small talk, you should remember one rule: **don't aim for brilliant, aim for nice**. When you start with easy, yet obvious comments and conversation starters, you put the other person at ease. This makes it easier for the person on the other end of the conversation to open up.

With that said, here is how to master the art of small talk:

Manage the Anxiety

We've covered this topic in previous steps. You are more likely to become anxious and nervous when you focus inwardly and have a fear of rejection. This may cause you to talk too much without allowing the other person a chance to comment or voice his or her opinion. Now you continue to blabber on and find it difficult to stay calm and composed. This is not an ideal approach to engage anyone in conversation.

This is why, even before you think of saying something to that seemingly interesting stranger, you should take some time to satiate the anxiety. You can do this by staying calm and thinking positively. Deep breathing and calming exercises will help you feel focused and foster a positive state of mind. You will learn how by following the methods detailed below.

(The following techniques are from my book *Social Skills*.)

"Here are the steps to calming your mind and refocusing your energy on being peaceful, stress-free and ready to engage other people in fun conversation:

6. Start out by taking a slow, long, and deep breath. As you take in the breath, feel your lungs being

filled from inside with all the anxiety and negativity.

7. Exhale slowly, feeling all the negativity flow out of your body.

8. Take one deep breath and feel the positive energy and 'goodness' fill your lungs.

9. Hold your breath for approximately 5 seconds and feel positive energy flowing into your body.

10. Breathe out again – feeling completely focused and happy.

This process (calming breath, negative energy out of your body, and feeling goodness returning back) will calm you by removing stress. Whether you realize it or not, practicing this type of breathing several times a day – especially when you feel the most anxious and troubled – will have a powerful **biofeedback affect.**

Biofeedback is used during meditation and breathing exercises to reduce vital signs in people that are having stressful situations. Studies show that this is highly effective at **controlling your emotions** and allowing you to regain mindfulness and focus."

Source: Reid Damon, *Social Skills*

We will finish the **Managing Anxiety** section by focusing on logic. To further reduce anxiety, ask yourself, "What's the worst that can happen?" An awkward conversation? Rejection from a stranger? In the bigger scheme of things — not a big deal!

Prepare

We have yet to master the conversation game at this point; therefore the confidence we need to strike up lasting conversations is still in its infancy. This is where we discuss the importance of preparation.

Preparation is key. You must prepare as you head to that networking event or party, or even as you wait to board the train. You can prepare by trying to come up with one or two things to talk about in the off chance that once you get through the introduction, the conversation streams run dry.

Preparation also means you should be purposeful about the conversation. If you approach small talk with the thought and belief that "this shall be so dull and pointless," this belief shall be self-fulfilling and the conversation you engage in shall be dull and pointless. Instead of considering small talk a pointless venture, acknowledge it for what it is, a way to build the foundation for authentic and deeper conversations and connections.

Master the Art of Introductions

Step 2 showed you how to make a proper introduction. To add on to what you learned in the previous step, great small-talkers have an uncanny mastery of introductions. In addition to offering your name, offer a great piece of information about yourself and do so in a manner that compels the person on the other end of the conversation to reciprocate. This is where the skills you learned in the art of introduction step come in handy.

Start on a Solid Footing

One of the many mistakes we commit when it comes to small talk is not giving the other person enough to work with. Let's use the example of when a stranger you are conversing with asks you what you do for a living. Instead of giving a one-worded answer "finance", give your response some meat. Otherwise, you will leave the other person scrambling for more questions, which ultimately, will kill the conversation. Give the other person tidbits he or she can use to keep the conversation going. For instance, you could have said, "I've been a certified financial advisor for the past five years. Have you seen the stock market lately? A lot of interesting things happening." Always give an opening.

Master Listening

We also talked about this in passing. If there is one thing we all love, it is talking about ourselves. Whenever you are talking to someone new, instead of making the conversation all about you, focus the majority of the conversation about the other person.

To do this, you need to develop your listening skills. The best way to develop great listening skills is to develop an intense level of curiosity in the other person, his or her response, and things of interests. This will help you learn what makes a person tick and when you find this, you can use it to start a deeper conversation. When you use one of the conversation starters/questions discussed in the last section, do so from a place of genuine interest. This will make the other person feel listened to, which will draw him or her out.

Action Step

When in a social situation such as a networking event (once you identify someone you would like to talk to, after the introduction), ease into small talk. Your observations and previous interaction will determine what type of topics to engage in – movies, television, technology, travel, sports, food, hobbies, family, etc.

Remember to have fun! Choose interesting and enjoyable topics. Besides the examples I have detailed below, search the internet for "conversation starters" to learn more small talk topics.

Examples:

What was the last movie you watched? How was it?
Where is the most beautiful place you have been?
Do you have any pets? What are their names?
Where do you spend most of your free time?
What did you do on your last vacation?
What weird or useless talent do you have?
What is your guilty pleasure?
What is the silliest fear you have?
What is your favorite movie genre?
What's your favorite show currently on TV?
What's the most addictive mobile game you have played?
What is the most useful app on your phone?

Do you experience phantom vibration? (Feeling your phone vibrate even though it didn't.)
What sports do you like to watch?
What is the most exciting sporting event you have attended?
What type of music do you enjoy listening to?
Do you like going to concerts? Why or why not?
What was the last concert you went to?
What is the last book you read?
What is the best restaurant in your area?
What is the fanciest restaurant you have eaten at?
What is your favorite item to drink (alcoholic or nonalcoholic)?
Do you prefer traveling alone or with a group?
Where is the most awe-inspiring place you have been?
Will technology save the human race or destroy it?
What technology from a science fiction movie would you most like to have?
What is your favorite luxury bag/piece of jewelry?
What is the craziest, most outrageous thing you want to achieve?
What is your favorite holiday?
Source: *250 Conversation Starters.* Conversation Starters World. Web. 5 September 2017.
https://conversationstartersworld.com/250-conversation-starters

Now that you have learned more conversational topics, learning how to keep a conversation going past the small talk is the next challenging step.

Notes:

_____

_____

_____

_____

_____

_____

_____

_____

_____

_____

_____

_____

_____

_____

_____

_____

_____

_____

_____

_____

_____

_____

_____

_____

_____

_____

_____

_____

_____ Keep practicing...

Step 4: Keep the Conversation Going Past the Pleasantries

One of the most terrifying things about being in a conversation, especially with strangers, is the awkward silence many of us experience after engaging in a fair amount of small talk.

The awkward silence is something that causes many not to take the plunge into conversation. Now that you have overcome the fear of talking to strangers, introduced yourself in the nicest way possible, and through conversation starters engaged in a fair amount of small talk, the next challenge is the challenge of never running out of things to say. How do we continue the conversation while keeping it interesting and flowing?

To overcome this problem, the first thing you need to understand is why the awkward silence happens, especially when you are conversing with strangers.

The awkward silence is internal because when you think you have run out of things to say that is exactly what is happening. You have activated a filter that sifts through what you think is good enough to say to a stranger thus limiting your choices.

This filter is almost nonexistent when you are conversing with people you know well. You can converse for hours about different unrelated topics without stressing over what to say next. Your "good enough for conversation" threshold is very low when speaking to a friend or acquaintance. If you feel like bringing up an interesting topic that pops into your mind, you just do.

Therein lies the answer to keeping a conversation going past the pleasantries. You must lose your inhibitions and not filter things out of your conversation. As long as a topic or thought is good enough to vocalize, do so. You need to learn how to adapt to conversations on the go, which you can do by removing this filter.

In addition to keeping the conversation going past the small talk and pleasantries, you need to be emotionally vulnerable. This does not mean you need to reveal your deepest darkest secret. All it means is that you have to lead first by opening up first. Be the first one to move the conversation past the pleasantries by sharing something personal. Here is why this is important.

You will pick up a few things about the other person when you are attentive. Even so, you cannot outright ask a stranger to tell you his or her darkest secrets. After all, you would not expect someone you just met to ask the same of you. You are likely to be more trusted when you are vulnerable and share something about yourself to the other person first. When people feel trusted, they reciprocate in kind. Because you have opened yourself up to them, they will open themselves up to you, which will take the conversation deeper.

Another way to take conversations past the pleasantries is to concentrate on the types of topics you bring up as you engage in small talk. In most cases, most of us have 10 or so questions we ask and when the stranger we are talking to answers most of these, an awkward silence ensues.

Here, you need to concentrate on using conversation prompts that call for more than one word answers. For instance, questions such as "how is work", "how are the kids" or "how have you been" will do very little to take the conversation past the surface. This is why you need to bring up weighty topics for discussion. Keep the conversation deep and interesting but avoid certain subject matters such as death or war. Our goal is to keep these conversations fun. Talking about death or war is certainly not fun.

Important and serious topics will foster a more interesting and engaging conversation. You will learn a lot about the other person by sharing impactful stories related to the topic in discussion. You will also have managed to take the conversation past the pleasantries.

Action Step

After engaging a stranger in small talk, drive the conversation deeper towards topics such as passions and interests, life philosophy and values, year goals, and other such topics that will excite the other person. This excitement will draw him or her into a deeper conversation.

Remember to listen keenly and to respond zealously. You can keep a conversation going after the pleasantries by continuing this type of dialogue while using the person's response to form other interesting questions and topics. This type of conversation shows a genuine interest in the person's life thus fostering the likelihood of a meaningful conversation.

Notes:

_____

_____

_____

_____

_____

_____

_____

_____

_____

_____

_____

_____

_____

_____

_____

_____

_____

_____

_____

_____

_____

_____

_____

_____

_____

_____ Keep practicing…

Step 5: Mirror and Match to Create Rapport With Strangers

If you are keen enough, you will have noted that when you and your closest friends get together, you tend to act the same and to some extent, even sound the same. This automatic chemistry response fosters oneness by making you appear the same.

Mirroring and matching, the aspect of copying the other's mannerisms, body language, and word cues, helps foster trust and establish rapport. Oxford Dictionary defines rapport as "a close and harmonious relationship in which the people or groups concerned understand each other's feelings or ideas and communicate well." As you can derive from this explanation, good rapport is a great way to strengthen your relationship with someone you just met.

Source: Oxford University Press. Web. 2 September 2017.
https://en.oxforddictionaries.com/definition/rapport

Mirroring is the aspect of matching or copying someone's behaviors and mannerisms. If you do this covertly, meaning you do it with respect, you will increase responsiveness by fostering the creation of positive feelings. **Matching** is similar to mirroring except that matching includes a built-in time lag. For instance, if the stranger you are talking to runs his or her hand through his or her hair, you have to wait several moments or minutes before doing the same. Practiced together, these Neuro-Linguistic Programming (NLP) techniques will make those around you comfortable. As stated earlier, we relate better with people we feel are like us. Mirroring and matching will help in this process.

The following strategies detailed below will guide you through Step 5. These methods are divided between **external messaging cues** (visual) and **language and vocal patterns** (auditory). These are simple things to keep mindful of when mirroring and matching while engaging in conversation.

1. Match External Messaging Cues

Here, you need to pay attention to three important visual cues:

Posture: Our attitudes and feelings often reflect our body language. By matching and mirroring someone's posture, you will begin to create a connection that helps you understand the person better. Remember to be covert and respectful throughout this process. Observe how the person on the other end of the conversation moves and then after 4-5 seconds mirror and match these movements to create a level of comfort.

Gestures: We use gestures to catalog and to describe our experiences. When matching gestures, nod or tilt your head similarly to how the stranger does, and if the gestures are expansive, restrictive, exaggerated, etc. covertly mirror those gestures.

Facial Expressions: The face has 43 muscles; this makes the face the most expressive part of the body. You can communicate so much without the need for words. Here, monitor facial expressions such as raised, lowered, or furrowed brows, a wrinkled bridge of the nose, a squared or tense jaw, etc. Another thing you may want to note is the blink rate of the person you are conversing with. Blink rate tends to correlate to the amount of mental stress we are under. A blink rate of 15 blinks or less per minute is ideal. More than 15 blinks show signs of anxiety and dishonesty.

2. Match Language and Vocal Patterns

Here, three important auditory patterns are discussed.

Tone/Inflection: Aspects of voice matching (tone, pitch, rate, volume, etc.) are best done indirectly. Be subtle when modifying your voice. Your "mirrored" voice should be more similar to the person you are conversing with but not drastically different from your own. Changing your voice in a drastic way will appear awkward and unnatural. The key is to be subtle.

Speech Rate: Your goal is to "mirror" the pace of speech of the individual you are speaking with as naturally and subtle as possible. You are not expected to alter your speech rate drastically. A slight modification is the goal. If you are a fast paced speaker talking to a more deliberate, slower speaker, you will slow your speech one notch to narrow the gap in tempo. Alternately, if you a deliberate, slower speaker conversing with a fast paced speaker, you will increase your tempo one notch.

***Sensory Predicates*:** Listen to verbal cues to help build rapport and foster a meaningful conversation. People tend to understand and communicate their experiences and thoughts using one of four types of sensory-based systems – visual, auditory, kinesthetic/feeling, and auditory-digital.

<u>Visual Predicates</u> include words and phrases such as: *show, dawn, look, appear, sunny, clear, dim, reveal, blurry, picture this, set eyes on, catch sight of, short-sighted, easy on the eyes, paint a picture, an eyeful, etc.*

<u>Auditory Predicates</u> may include terms and phrases such as: *sound(s), harmonize, hear, tell, listen, resonate, give me your ear, rings a bell, tune in/out, quiet as a mouse, voiced an opinion, clear as a bell, loud-and-clear, tune in/out, on another note, etc.*

<u>Kinesthetic/Feeling Predicates</u> include words and phrases such as: *touch, feel, grasp, smooth, hard, concrete, unfeeling, scrape, heated debate, sharp as a tack, get in touch with, make contact, tap into, throw out, hand-in-hand,* etc.

<u>Auditory Digital Predicates</u> may include word and phrases such as: *sense, process, change, think, know, learn, decide, consider, perceive, conceive,*

understand, experience, motivate, figure it out, make sense of, pay attention to, word-for-word, etc.

You can incorporate these predicates into your speech once you understand how a person thinks and talks. This strategy will subconsciously foster a natural connection with the other individual.

"How can you use this in mirroring and matching to create rapport? When we 'speak the same language', we have a more solid foundation on which to build trust. For example, a client may say to you, '*I like the **look** of the contract. The bottom-line is **clear** and your plan is **focused**.*' You might reply with something like, '*I'm glad that I was able to **paint a clear picture** of the project; let's **see** how we can work together toward a common **vision** for the work.*' The underlying system of communication is overwhelmingly visible... *See* what I mean?"

Source: *The Art of Building Rapport, Part I: Mirroring & Matching.* Coaching and the Journey. Web. 10 October 2017.
https://coachingandthejourney.wordpress.com/2012/10/22/the-art-of-building-rapport

Action Step

The next time you engage a stranger in a conversation, start matching and mirroring the person starting from the introductions. For example, mirror someone's soft gaze, smile, handshake, and then covertly match and mirror his or her body posture and body language. Remember to have fun and be respectful!

Notes:

_____

_____

_____

_____

_____

_____

_____

_____

_____

_____

_____

_____

_____

_____

_____

_____

_____

_____

_____

_____

_____

_____

_____

_____

_____

Keep practicing...

Step 6: Learn How to Turn Strangers Into Friends

The greatest of things come to those who are willing to risk rejection and failure. The fear of rejection is the very thing that has been keeping you from creating lasting friendships and relationships with strangers. Now that you have implemented steps 1 through 5, you have overcome this fear. Congratulations! You are now ready for the challenge of turning one off chance conversation with a stranger into a lasting friendship. Here is how to do that:

Build on the Commonalities

At this point, we shall assume that the stranger you want to turn into a friend is someone you have engaged in small talk, and after deepening the conversation, matching and mirroring, have decided that this person is someone worth making a friend.

To keep this conversation going and the friendship flourishing, you can build on commonalities. For instance, if both you and the stranger/acquaintance like hiking, and you and several other friends have planned a hike in the coming weeks or month, you can casually invite this person and then continue deepening the conversation on this point of mutual interest. Because the person likes hiking, he or she is more likely to say yes, and this will offer you a chance to meet the person for a second time. This future interaction will cement the acquaintance and turn it into a budding friendship.

Don't Forget the Contact Information

After having a great first conversation with someone you just met, before you go your separate ways, read the situation. If you feel that the person had a great time conversing with you (especially if, in the earlier example, the person agrees to come for the planned hike), take the initiative and ask for contact information.

Having contact information of your "new friend" is going to make communication easier for when you plan to meet up again. When it comes to asking for contact information, just be direct. Say something like, "I had so much fun chatting with you. Before you go, let's exchange numbers so we can get together and chat more about that hike."

Be Friendly

In more than one occasion, we have indicated that acquaintances feel more attracted to us, and thus more open to friendships, if we are open and vulnerable at a personal level. This is what we mean by being friendly. Once you navigate through steps 1-5 of connecting with a stranger, that person is no longer a stranger, he or she is an acquaintance, which is a step away from friendship. Treat such a person as you would treat a friend, which means you should embark on creating a level of honest communication and familiarity while discussing and acting on mutual interests.

Action Step

As you end an interesting conversation with a stranger, ask for contact information so you can reach out later and continue the conversation or engage in something of mutual interest (ie. shopping, golfing, dancing, book club, etc).

Notes:

_____

_____

_____

_____

_____

_____

_____

_____

_____

_____

_____

_____

_____

_____

_____

_____

_____

_____

_____

_____

_____

_____

_____

_____

_____

Keep practicing…

Step 7: Learn How to Become the Center of Attention

Now that you are coming to the end of this 7 step guide, you need to learn one more skill: how to become the center of attention. If you have noticed, the first 6 steps of this guide have a central theme: outward concentration on the person at the other end of the conversation.

Naturally, there are instances where you will want to hog attention when in a social situation. For instance, if we go with our hiking example from step 6, when you, your new friend and other friends do finally go for that hike, you may want to be the center of attention so you can keep the conversation going and keep your new friend from feeling left out. Here are several ways to do that:

Assume a Central Position

If you are attending a social gathering, one effective way to attract attention is to stand or sit at a prominent position where attention is centrally focused. Perhaps stand in the center of the room and then ask your friends to join you there or seat yourself in the middle of the table. This will make you appear friendly and approachable, which means strangers will feel drawn to you.

Move Periodically

Continuing with the social gathering example, even after assuming a central location, do not cement yourself there, which is what many of us tend to do. Instead, move positions at intervals of 15-30 minutes. This ensures you interact with as many people as possible, which also means you will end up attracting a lot of good attention.

Be the Conversation Starter

We have talked about the importance of being the bold one. You have to realize that most people shy away from starting a conversation. Therefore, if you are the one starting them, you will be "the one" reaching out to those around you. You will automatically become the center of attention. Moreover, remember to follow the rules of starting a conversation: keep the conversation light, and when you stumble upon someone or a group of interesting people, deepen the conversation, and rope in more people into the conversation.

Action Step

Work on your confidence. Being the center of attention demands that you be confident because it means the spotlight shall be on you. If you are not confident, having the spotlight on you may breed social anxiety where you are fearful of negative judgment by those around you. Confidence is built through positive thinking and practice, practice, and more practice.

Notes:

_____
_____
_____
_____
_____
_____
_____
_____
_____
_____
_____
_____
_____
_____
_____
_____
_____
_____
_____
_____
_____
_____
_____
_____
_____

Keep practicing…

Conclusion

Thank you again for reading this book!

I hope this book was able to help you to learn to have a conversation with anyone while having fun throughout. Enjoying the process is an important factor to your success.

After implementing these 7 steps, you will come out the other end a better conversationalist. As you implement each of these steps, take your time and do not rush or pressure yourself into doing something you are not ready to do yet. Remember this is supposed to be FUN! Build your confidence, practice, and have FUN!

Once you have become a better conversationalist, the next step is to challenge yourself in something else. Have you ever wanted to be a better dancer? Do you have a bucket list of things you want to accomplish in life? From taking a dance class to learning to fly a plane, do whatever your heart desires. Take the steps to make your dreams a reality.

Enjoy every day. Live life your way!

Thank you and good luck!

46145413R00069

Printed in Poland
by Amazon Fulfillment
Poland Sp. z o.o., Wrocław